Your Daily Success Pill

365 quotes on success
to inspire, enlighten and
ignite your drive.

Copyright 2017 © Your Daily Pill

All Rights Reserved

Spread across the following 365 pages are quotes on **success** – one for each day of the year. Think of each as your **daily success pill** intended to inspire, enlighten and ignite your drive.

Begin with the end in mind.

Stephen Covey

It is hard to fail, but it is worse never to have tried to succeed.

Theodore Roosevelt

All you need is the plan,
the road map, and the courage
to press on to your destination.

Earl Nightingale

Achievement is talent plus preparation

Malcolm Gladwell

Things work out best
for those who make the best
of how things work out.

John Wooden

Doubt kills more dreams
than failure ever will.

Suzy Kassem

We may encounter many defeats but we must not be defeated.

Maya Angelou

Success is like a liberation
or the first phrase of a love story.

Jeanne Moreau

One worthwhile task carried
to a successful conclusion
is worth half-a-hundred
half-finished tasks.

Malcolm S. Forbes

What you lack in talent can be made up with desire, hustle and giving 110% all the time.

Don Zimmer

Every successful person I have heard of has done the best he could with the conditions as he found them, and not waited until next year for better.

E. W. Howe

We generate fears while we sit.
We overcome them by action.

Dr. Henry Link

Success is liking yourself,
liking what you do,
and liking how you do it.

Maya Angelou

Don't judge each day
by the harvest you reap
but by the seeds you plant.

Robert Louis Stevenson

People who succeed at the highest level are not lucky; they're doing something differently than everyone else.

Tony Robbins

Accepting oneself
does not preclude
an attempt to become better.

Flannery O'Connor

There is only one success –
to be able to spend your life
in your own way.

Christopher Morley

Failures are the stairs we climb to reach success.

Roy T. Bennett

Successful people are the ones who are breaking the rules.

Seth Godin

Success is not built on success.
It's built on failure.
It's built on frustration.
Sometimes it's built
on catastrophe.

Sumner Redstone

Satisfaction lies in the effort,
not in the attainment,
full effort is full victory.

Mahatma Gandhi

I am thankful for all of those who said NO to me. It's because of them I'm doing it myself.

Albert Einstein

Forget all the reasons
it won't work
and believe the one reason
that it will.

Anonymous

All progress takes place
outside the comfort zone.

Michael John Bobak

Be content to act,
and leave the talking to others.

Baltasa

Who you are tomorrow
begins with what you do today.

Tim Fargo

The difference between a successful person and others is not a lack of strength, not a lack of knowledge, but rather a lack of will.

Vince Lombardi

Failure is instructive. The person who really thinks learns quite as much from his failures as from his successes.

John Dewey

The first man gets the oyster,
the second man gets the shell.

Andrew Carnegie

Whatever you are, be a good one.

Abraham Lincoln

The only place
where success comes before work
is in the dictionary.

Vidal Sassoon

The two most important requirements for major success are: first, being in the right place at the right time, and second, doing something about it.

Ray Kroc

Before everything else, getting ready is the secret of success.

Henry Ford

For success, attitude is equally as important as ability.

Walter Scott

Any coward can fight a battle
when he's sure of winning;
but give me the man
who has the pluck to fight
when he's sure of losing.

George Eliot

It's failure that gives you the proper perspective on success.

Ellen DeGeneres

Failure is a bend in the road,
not the end of the road.
Learn from failure
and keep moving forward.

Roy T. Bennett

Along with success comes a reputation for wisdom.

Euripides

If A is a success in life,
then A equals x plus y plus z.
Work is x; y is play; and z is
keeping your mouth shut.

Albert Einstein

Every achievement,
big or small,
begins in your mind.

Mary Kay Ash

You must expect great things of yourself before you can do them.

Michael Jordan

Without self-discipline,
success is impossible, period.

Lou Holtz

It's not whether you get knocked down, it's whether you get up.

Vince Lombardi

Our greatest glory
is not in never falling,
but in rising every time we fall.

Oliver Goldsmith

Life isn't about finding yourself.
Life is about creating yourself.

George Bernard Shaw

Don't let what you cannot do interfere with what you can do.

John Wooden

Success will be within your reach only when you start reaching out for it.

Stephen Richards

If opportunity doesn't knock,
build a door.

Milton Berle

One of the secrets to success
is ideas mixed with inspiration.

Jim Rohn

Champions do not become champions when they win an event, but in the hours, weeks, and months, and years they spend preparing for it. The victorious performance itself is merely a demonstration of their championship character.

Michael Jordan

No one is going to hand me success. I must go out and get it myself. That's why I'm here. To dominate. To conquer. Both the world, and myself.

Anonymous

Keep your face
always toward the sunshine –
and shadows will fall behind you.

Walt Whitman

Enjoying success requires
the ability to adapt.
Only by being open to change
will you have a true opportunity
to get the most from your talent.

Nolan Ryan

Doing the best at this moment puts you in the best place for the next moment.

Oprah Winfrey

Being defeated is often a temporary condition. Giving up is what makes it permanent.

Marilyn vos Savant

The first step toward success is taken when you refuse to be a captive of the environment in which you first find yourself.

Mark Caine

Eighty percent of success
is showing up.

Woody Allen

Knowing is not enough;
we must apply.
Wishing is not enough;
we must do.

Johann Wolfgang Von Goethe

The secret to success is to know something nobody else knows.

Aristotle Onassis

Success isn't just about what you accomplish in your life; it's about what you inspire others to do.

Anonymous

Success is that old ABC:
Ability, Breaks and Courage.

Charles Luckman

Everyone has talent. What is rare is the courage to follow the talent to the dark place where it leads.

Erica Jong

It is literally true that you can succeed best and quickest by helping others to succeed.

Napoleon Hill

If I cannot do great things, I can do small things in a great way.

Martin Luther King Jr.

Once we believe in ourselves,
we can risk curiosity, wonder,
spontaneous delight,
or any experience
that reveals the human spirit.

E. E. Cummings

What would you attempt to do if you knew you would not fail?

Robert Schuller

The only time you fail is when you fall down and stay down.

Stephen Richards

Everybody's got a past.
The past does not equal
the future unless you live there.

Tony Robbins

I find my greatest pleasure,
and so my reward,
in the work that precedes
what the world calls success.

Thomas A. Edison

The best revenge
is massive success.

Frank Sinatra

There are no speed limits on the road to success.

David W. Johnson

If you hang out with chickens,
you're going to cluck
and if you hang out with eagles,
you're going to fly.

Steve Maraboli

You will find the key to success under the alarm clock.

Benjamin Franklin

Success is not the key to happiness. Happiness is the key to success. If you love what you are doing, you will be successful.

Albert Schweitzer

Fall seven times
and stand up eight.

Japanese Proverb

Only those who dare to fail greatly can ever achieve greatly.

Robert F. Kennedy

A journey of a thousand miles begins with a single step.

Lao Tzu

Success is a journey, not a destination. The doing is often more important than the outcome.

Arthur Ashe

I arise full of eagerness and energy, knowing well what achievement lies ahead of me.

Zane Grey

People rarely succeed unless they have fun in what they are doing.

Dale Carnegie

How many a man has thrown up his hands at a time when a little more effort, a little more patience would have achieved success.

Elbert Hubbard

Most of the successful people I've known are the ones who do more listening than talking.

Bernard Baruch

Don't let yesterday
take up too much of today.

Will Rogers

To be successful you must accept all challenges that come your way. You can't just accept the ones you like.

Mike Gafka

When your work speaks for itself,
don't interrupt.

Henry J. Kaiser

A strong, positive self-image is the best possible preparation for success.

Joyce Brothers

The road to success is dotted with many tempting parking spaces.

Will Rogers

Frustration, although quite painful at times, is a very positive and essential part of success.

Bo Bennett

Accept responsibility for your life.
Know that it is you who will get
you where you want to go,
no one else.

Les Brown

What the mind can conceive,
it can achieve.

Napoleon Hill

When your life flashes before your eyes, make sure you've got plenty to watch.

Anonymous

I owe my success to having listened respectfully to the very best advice, and then going away and doing the exact opposite.

G. K. Chesterton

Trust because you are willing to accept the risk, not because it's safe or certain.

Anonymous

That man is a success
who has lived well,
laughed often and loved much.

Robert Louis Stevenson

Many of life's failures are people who did not realize how close they were to success when they gave up.

Thomas A. Edison

Expect the best.
Prepare for the worst.
Capitalize on what comes.

Zig Ziglar

Definiteness of purpose is the starting point of all achievement.

W. Clement Stone

Courage is being scared to death, but saddling up anyway.

John Wayne

Successful people do what unsuccessful people are not willing to do. Don't wish it were easier; wish you were better.

Jim Rohn

Every day I get up and look through the Forbes list of the richest people in America. If I'm not there, I go to work.

Vinnie Rege

The secret to success:
find out where people are going
and get there first

Mark Twain

Thirteen virtues necessary for true success: temperance, silence, order, resolution, frugality, industry, sincerity, justice, moderation, cleanliness, tranquility, chastity, and humility.

Benjamin Franklin

You have to do your own growing
no matter how tall
your grandfather was.

Abraham Lincoln

If you can dream it, you can do it.

Walt Disney

All great achievements
require time.

Maya Angelou

Use what talents you possess; the woods would be very silent if no birds sang there except those that sang best.

Henry Van Dyke

Take up one idea.
Make that one idea your life –
think of it, dream of it, live on
that idea. Let the brain, muscles,
nerves, every part of your body,
be full of that idea, and just leave
every other idea alone.
This is the way to success.

Swami Vivekananda

All meaningful and lasting change starts first in your imagination and then works its way out.

Albert Einstein

I do not think that there is any other quality so essential to success of any kind as the quality of perseverance. It overcomes almost everything, even nature.

John D. Rockefeller

It's not about how much you do, but how much love you put into what you do that counts.

Mother Teresa

I don't believe in failure. It is not failure if you enjoyed the process.

Oprah Winfrey

Ask yourself the secret of your success. Listen to your answer, and practice it.

Richard Bach

Whether you think you can or think you can't, you're right.

Henry Ford

Success is the sum of small efforts, repeated day-in and day-out.

Robert Collier

I attribute my success to this:
I never gave or took any excuse.

Florence Nightingale

Act the way you'd like to be and soon you'll be the way you act.

Leonard Cohen

Some people dream of great accomplishments, while others stay awake and do them.

Anonymous

If a man will begin with certainties, he shall end in doubts, but if he will content to begin with doubts, he shall end in certainties.

Francis Bacon

I believe that if one always
looked at the skies,
one would end up with wings.

Gustave Flaubert

I find that the harder I work, the more luck I seem to have.

Thomas Jefferson

There are two secrets to success:
1. Never tell everything you know.

Steven Shelton

I dwell in possibility.

Emily Dickinson

If you really look closely, most overnight successes took a long time.

Steve Jobs

Our greatest fear should not be of failure but of succeeding at things in life that don't really matter.

Francis Chan

The great secret of success
is to go through life as a man
who never gets used to failing.

Albert Schweitzer

Success is not final; failure is not fatal: it is the courage to continue that counts.

Winston Churchill

Nobody ever wrote down a plan to be broke, fat, lazy, or stupid. Those things are what happen when you don't have a plan.

Larry Winget

Rarely have I seen a situation where doing less than the other guy is a good strategy.

Jimmy Spithill

The secret of success is to do the common thing uncommonly well.

John D. Rockefeller Jr.

If you don't build your dream,
someone else will hire you
to help them build theirs.

Dhirubhai Ambani

Success is just a war of attrition. Sure, there's an element of talent you should probably possess. But if you just stick around long enough, eventually something is going to happen.

Dax Shepard

Character cannot be developed in ease and quiet. Only through experience of trial and suffering can the soul be strengthened, ambition inspired, and success achieved.

Helen Keller

Your positive action
combined with positive thinking
results in success.

Shiv Khera

In life, we must first learn
to crawl, then stand, then walk,
then run, and only then, fly.
We cannot crawl into flying.

Anonymous

Trade your expectation for appreciation and the world changes instantly.

Tony Robbins

If you are not willing to risk the usual you will have to settle for the ordinary.

Jim Rohn

If you are working on something
that you really care about,
you don't have to be pushed.
The vision pulls you.

Steve Jobs

Success comes from aspiration, desperation, perspiration, and inspiration!

Denise Austin

Every failure is a step to success.

William Whewell

The fastest way to succeed is to look as if you're playing by somebody else's rules, while quietly playing by your own.

Michael Korda

The superior man
makes the difficulty to be
overcome his first interest;
success only comes later.

Confucius

In order to succeed,
we must first believe that we can.

Nikos Kazantzakis

Self-belief and hard work
will always earn you success.

Virat Kohli

There is no success without hardship.

Sophocles

Don't let the fear of losing
be greater than the excitement
of winning.

Robert Kiyosaki

Success is a state of mind.
If you want success, start thinking
of yourself as a success.

Joyce Brothers

Success usually comes
to those who are too busy
to be looking for it.

Henry David Thoreau

I never dreamed about success,
I worked for it.

Estee Lauder

Do not be embarrassed
by your failures,
learn from them and start again.

Richard Branson

When you can't change
the direction of the wind,
just adjust your sails.

H. Jackson Brown Jr

We need to accept that we won't always make the right decisions, that we'll screw up royally sometimes - understanding that failure is not the opposite of success, it's part of success.

Arianna Huffington

Argue for your limitations,
and sure enough they're yours.

Richard Bach

Winners never quit
and quitters never win.

Vince Lombardi

We must radiate success before it will come to us. We must first become mentally, from an attitude standpoint, the people we wish to become.

Earl Nightingale

The secret of success is
to be in harmony with existence,
to be always calm to let each wave
of life wash us a little
farther up the shore.

Cyril Connolly

The three great essentials
to achieve anything worthwhile
are, first, hard work;
second, stick-to-itiveness;
third, common sense.

Thomas A. Edison

Men are born to succeed,
not to fail.

Henry David Thoreau

One thing is forever good;
That one thing is Success.

Ralph Waldo Emerson

There are three ingredients
in the good life:
learning, earning and yearning.

Christopher Morley

Whosoever desires constant success must change his conduct with the times.

Niccolò Machiavelli

Success is following the pattern of life one enjoys most.

Al Capp

Those who have succeeded at anything and don't mention luck are kidding themselves.

Larry King

Define success on your own terms, achieve it by your own rules, and build a life you're proud to live.

Anne Sweeney

After my spectacular failures,
I could not be satisfied
with an ordinary success.

Mason Cooley

The secret of success is this:
there is no secret of success.

Elbert Hubbard

You don't pay the price
for success,
you enjoy the benefits of success.

Zig Ziglar

When I was young,
I observed that nine out of ten
things I did were failures.
So I did ten times more work.

George Bernard Shaw

To succeed, you need to find something to hold on to, something to motivate you, something to inspire you.

Tony Dorsett

If you want to be successful,
it's just this simple.
Know what you are doing.
Love what you are doing.
And believe in what you are doing.

Will Rogers

Those who dare to fail miserably can achieve greatly.

John F. Kennedy

You may be disappointed
if you fail, but you are doomed
if you don't try.

Beverly Sills

Success is the child of audacity.

Benjamin Disraeli

Success seems to be largely a matter of hanging on after others have let go.

William Feather

Talent is a gift, but you can only succeed with hard work.

Jean Beliveau

A goal is a dream with a deadline.

Napoleon Hill

Put your heart, mind, and soul into even your smallest acts. This is the secret of success.

Sivananda

Fortune sides with him who dares.

Virgil

Men who try to do something and fail are infinitely better than those who try to do nothing and succeed.

Lloyd Jones

The key to success is failure.

Michael Jordan

The trees that are slow to grow bear the best fruit.

Moliere

Whatever the mind can conceive and believe, it can achieve.

Napoleon Hill

Each success only buys
an admission ticket
to a more difficult problem.

Henry A. Kissinger

Never give up on what you really want to do. The person with big dreams is more powerful than one with all the facts.

H. Jackson Brown Jr

Twenty years from now
you will be more disappointed
by the things that you didn't do
than by the ones you did do.
So throw off the bowlines.
Catch the trade winds in your
sails. Explore. Dream. Discover.

Mark Twain

A successful man is one who can lay a firm foundation with the bricks others have thrown at him.

David Brinkley

The road to success is wherever people need another road.

Robert Breault

It's just as difficult
to overcome success
as it is to overcome failure.

William Walton

That some achieve great success,
is proof to all that others
can achieve it as well.

Abraham Lincoln

The secret of success is making your vocation your vacation.

Mark Twain

Some people want it to happen, some wish it would happen, others make it happen.

Michael Jordan

Your goal should be out of reach
but not out of sight.

Anita DeFrantz

Success isn't permanent and failure isn't fatal.

Mike Ditka

Successful and unsuccessful people do not vary greatly in their abilities. They vary in their desires to reach their potential.

John Maxwell

Real success doesn't care how you get there.

Ernie J Zelinski

It is never too late to be what you might have been.

George Eliot

Don't ask what the world needs. Ask what makes you come alive and go do it. Because what the world needs is more people who have come alive.

Howard Thurman

The secret of achievement is to hold a picture of a successful outcome in mind.

Henry David Thoreau

Failures are finger posts
on the road to achievement.

C. S. Lewis

A No. 2 pencil and a dream
can take you anywhere.

Joyce Meyer

Some succeed because they are destined to, but most succeed because they are determined to.

Henry Van Dyke

Action is the foundational key to all success.

Pablo Picasso

There are victories
of the soul and spirit.
Sometimes, even if you lose,
you win.

Elie Wiesel

If your ship doesn't come in, swim out to meet it!

Jonathan Winters

Always bear in mind that your own resolution to succeed is more important than any one thing.

Abraham Lincoln

You have to learn the rules of the game. And then you have to play better than anyone else.

Albert Einstein

A man is a success if he gets up in the morning and gets to bed at night, and in between he does what he wants to do.

Bob Dylan

Opportunity is missed by most people because it is dressed in overalls and looks like work.

Thomas Edison

Try not to become
a man of success.
Rather become a man of value.

Albert Einstein

The more you think and talk
about your goals,
the more positive and enthusiastic
you become.

Billy Cox

Each new day is a blank page
in the diary of your life.
The secret of success
is in turning that diary
into the best story
you possibly can.

Douglas Pagels

The only limit
to our realization of tomorrow
will be our doubts of today.

Franklin D. Roosevelt

There is no such thing as failure, only results.

Tony Robbins

The ladder of success is never crowded at the top.

Napoleon Hill

Failure is the condiment
that gives success its flavor.

Truman Capote

The successful warrior
is the average man,
with laser-like focus.

Bruce Lee

Success is not how high you have climbed, but how you make a positive difference to the world.

Roy T. Bennett

Too many of us are not living our dreams because we are living our fears.

Les Brown

Do your work with your whole heart, and you will succeed – there's so little competition.

Elbert Hubbard

The greater the obstacle,
the more glory in overcoming it.

Moliere

To succeed, it is necessary to accept the world as it is and rise above it.

Michael Korda

Our doubts are traitors and make us lose the good we oft might win by fearing to attempt.

William Shakespeare

A person with a new idea is a crank until the idea succeeds.

Mark Twain

No student ever attains very eminent success by simply doing what is required of him:
it is the amount and excellence of what is over and above the required, that determines the greatness of ultimate distinction.

Charles Kendall Adams

Success is a little
like wrestling a gorilla.
You don't quit when you're tired.
You quit when the gorilla is tired.

Robert Strauss

I have not failed. I've just found 10,000 ways that won't work.

Thomas A. Edison

The greater the artist, the greater the doubt. Perfect confidence is granted to the less talented as a consolation prize.

Robert Hughes

I play to win, whether during practice or a real game.
And I will not let anything get in the way of me and my competitive enthusiasm to win.

Michael Jordan

Everything you want is out there waiting for you to ask. Everything you want also wants you. But you have to take action to get it.

Jack Canfield

Obstacles are those frightful things you see when you take your eyes off your goal.

Henry Ford

You know you are on the road to success if you would do your job, and not be paid for it.

Oprah Winfrey

I'm a success today because I had
a friend who believed in me
and I didn't have the heart
to let him down.

Abraham Lincoln

To succeed in life, you need three things: a wishbone, a backbone and a funnybone.

Reba McEntire

My philosophy is that not only are you responsible for your life, but doing the best at this moment puts you in the best place for the next moment.

Oprah Winfrey

Life is like photography.
You need the negatives
to develop.

Anonymous

Success is nothing more
than a few simple disciplines,
practiced every day.

Jim Rohn

Success is where preparation and opportunity meet.

Bobby Unser

The secret of success in life
is for a man to be ready for his
opportunity when it comes.

Benjamin Disraeli

The thing always happens that you really believe in; and the belief in a thing makes it happen.

Frank Lloyd Wright

You learn more from failure than from success. Don't let it stop you. Failure builds character.

Anonymous

Your attitude is either the lock on, or the key to the door of your success.

Denis Waitley

To be successful, you have to have your heart in your business, and your business in your heart.

Sr. Thomas Watson

The man who has confidence in himself gains the confidence of others.

Hasidic Proverb

If you find a path
with no obstacles, it probably
doesn't lead anywhere.

Frank A. Clark

The universe doesn't give you what you ask for with your thoughts – it gives you what you demand with your actions.

Steve Maraboli

Two roads diverged in a wood and I – I took the one less traveled by, and that has made all the difference.

Robert Frost

Winners are not afraid of losing. But losers are. Failure is part of the process of success. People who avoid failure also avoid success.

Robert T. Kiyosaki

You might well remember that nothing can bring you success but yourself.

Napoleon Hill

No matter how many mistakes you make or how slow you progress, you are still way ahead of everyone who isn't trying.

Tony Robbins

Big pay and little responsibility are circumstances seldom found together.

Napoleon Hill

It is better to fail in originality than to succeed in imitation.

Herman Melville

Failure is acceptable,
but not trying
is a whole different ball park.

Michael Jordan

Those who don't jump
will never fly.

Leena Ahmad Almashat

I failed my way to success.

Thomas Edison

People don't have to believe in you for you to succeed. Just work hard, when you succeed, they will believe.

Stephen Keshi

Impatience never commanded success.

Edwin Hubbel Chapin

I can accept failure,
everyone fails at something.
But I can't accept not trying.

Michael Jordan

A minute's success
pays the failure of years.

Robert Browning

The only thing that stands between you and your dream is the will to try and the belief that it is actually possible.

Joel Brown

Good, better, best.
Never let it rest.
Until your good is better
and your better is best.

Tim Duncan

The successful man is the one who finds out what is the matter with his business
before his competitors do.

Roy L. Smith

The secret of success in life
is known only by those
who have not succeeded.

John Churton Collins

And will you succeed?
Yes indeed, yes indeed!
Ninety-eight and three-quarters
percent guaranteed!

Dr. Seuss

You're not obligated to win.
You're obligated to keep trying
to do the best you can every day.

Marian Wright Edelman

Success is steady progress toward one's personal goals.

Jim Rohn

Don't be afraid to give up the good to go for the great.

John D. Rockefeller

We cannot change the cards
we are dealt,
just how we play the hand.

Randy Pausch

Success is the doing,
not the getting;
in the trying, not the triumph.

Zig Ziglar

The thermometer of success
is merely the jealousy
of the malcontents.

Salvador Dalí

My great concern is not whether you have failed, but whether you are content with your failure.

Abraham Lincoln

Most people fail in life because they major in minor things.

Tony Robbins

There's a word for a writer who never gives up: published.

J.A. Konrath

If you genuinely want something,
don't wait for it –
teach yourself to be impatient.

Gurbaksh Chahal

Kites rise highest
against the wind, not with it.

Winston S. Churchill

It had long since come to my attention that people of accomplishment rarely sat back and let things happen to them. They went out
and happened to things.

Leonardo da Vinci

Don't be distracted by criticism.
Remember – the only taste of
success some people get
is to take a bite out of you.

Zig Ziglar

If you're going through hell, keep going.

Winston Churchill

Never was anything great achieved without danger.

Niccolò Machiavelli

Success is not the position where you stand, but the direction in which you look.

Anonymous

Some of us have great runways already built for us.
If you have one, take off.
But if you don't have one, realize it is your responsibility to grab a shovel and build one for yourself and for those who will follow after you.

Amelia Earhart

Success does not consist
in never making mistakes
but in never making the same one
a second time.

George Bernard Shaw

When you fail, that is when you get closer to success.

Stephen Richards

If you aren't making any mistakes, it's a sure sign you're playing it too safe.

John C. Maxwell

I cannot give you the formula for success, but I can give you the formula for failure – It is:
Try to please everybody.

Herbert Bayard Swope

The middle of every successful project looks like a disaster.

Rosabeth Moss Kanter

Follow your bliss
and the universe will open doors
where there were only walls.

        Joseph Campbell

Identify your problems
but give your power and energy
to solutions.

Tony Robbins

Develop success from failures. Discouragement and failure are two of the surest stepping stones to success.

Dale Carnegie

One of the rewards of success is freedom, the ability to do whatever you like.

Sting

The starting point of all achievement is desire.

Napoleon Hill

Some people say I have attitude – maybe I do... but I think you have to. You have to believe in yourself when no one else does – that makes you a winner right there.

Venus Williams

One sound idea is all that you need to achieve success.

Napoleon Hill

You are never too old
to set another goal
or to dream a new dream.

C. S. Lewis

Success to me is having
ten honeydew melons and eating
only the top half of each slice.

Barbra Streisand

There are no secrets to success. It is the result of preparation, hard work, and learning from failure.

Colin Powell

Success is walking from failure to failure with no loss of enthusiasm.

Winston Churchill

Failure is the key to success; each mistake teaches us something.

Morihei Ueshiba

Stay committed to your decisions, but stay flexible in your approach.

Tony Robbins

All you need in this life is ignorance and confidence; then success is sure.

Mark Twain

There is no failure
except in no longer trying.

Elbert Hubbard

Curious that we spend more time congratulating people who have succeeded than encouraging people who have not.

Neil deGrasse Tyson

Nothing can stop the man with the right mental attitude from achieving his goal; nothing on earth can help the man with the wrong mental attitude.

Thomas Jefferson

Supreme excellence consists of breaking the enemy's resistance without fighting.

Sun Tzu

Challenges are what make life interesting and overcoming them is what makes life meaningful.

Joshua J. Marine

The whole secret of a successful life is to find out what is one's destiny to do, and then do it.

Henry Ford

If you care at all, you'll get some results. If you care enough, you'll get incredible results.

Edward Simmons

Success means we go to sleep at night knowing that our talents and abilities were used in a way that served others.

Marianne Williamson

You learn nothing form your successes except to think too much of yourself. It is from failure that all growth comes, provided you can recognize it, admit it, learn from it, rise above it, and then try again.

Dee Hock

If you have the will to win,
you have achieved half your
success; if you don't, you have
achieved half your failure.

David Ambrose

It is not the going out of port,
but the coming in,
that determines the success
of a voyage.

Henry Ward Beecher

To succeed in business,
to reach the top, an individual
must know all it is possible to
know about that business.

J. Paul Getty

I've failed over and over and over
again in my life
and that is why I succeed.

Michael Jordan

Do one thing every day
that scares you.

Anonymous

Success is blocked by concentrating on it and planning for it... Success is shy – it won't come out while you're watching.

Tennessee Williams

Success is how high you bounce when you hit bottom.

George S. Patton

The distance between
insanity and genius
is measured only by success.

Bruce Feirstein

Our business in life is not to succeed, but to continue to fail in good spirits.

Robert Louis Stevenson

The only way to do great work is to love what you do.
If you haven't found it yet, keep looking. Don't settle.

Steve Jobs

The measure of success is not whether you have a tough problem to deal with,
but whether it is the same problem you had last year.

John Foster Dulles

People who are unable to motivate themselves must be content with mediocrity, no matter how impressive their other talents.

Andrew Carnegie

We must walk consciously only
part way toward our goal,
and then leap in the dark
to our success.

Henry David Thoreau

Failure defeats losers,
failure inspires winners.

Robert T. Kiyosaki

Success is counted sweetest by those who never succeed.

Emily Dickinson

First they ignore you.
Then they laugh at you.
Then they fight you.
Then you win.

Mahatma Gandhi

Judge your success by what you had to give up in order to get it.

Dalai Lama

Failure will never overtake me if my determination to succeed is strong enough.

Og Mandino

Excellence is doing ordinary things extraordinarily well.

John W. Gardner

The road to success
and the road to failure
are almost exactly the same.

Colin R. Davis

Never limit yourself because of others' limited imagination; never limit others because of your own limited imagination.

Mae Jemison

The people who are crazy enough to think they can change the world, are the ones who do.

Steve Jobs

The line between
failure and success is so fine...
that we are often on the line
and do not know it.

Elbert Hubbard

We succeed in enterprises
which demand the positive
qualities we possess,
but we excel in those which can
also make use of our defects.

Alexis de Tocqueville

There are two types of people
who will tell you that you cannot
make a difference in this world:
those who are afraid to try
and those who are afraid
you will succeed.

Ray Goforth

Change can either challenge or threaten us. Your beliefs pave your way to success or block you.

Marsha Sinetar

Think of yourself as on the threshold of unparalleled success. A whole, clear, glorious life lies before you. Achieve! Achieve!

Andrew Carnegie

Dreams come true; without that possibility, nature would not incite us to have them.

John Updike

Every man's responsibility
is his own responsibility.

Abraham Lincoln

You may only succeed if you desire succeeding; you may only fail if you do not mind failing.

Philippos

Light tomorrow with today.

Elizabeth Barrett Browning

If you wish to succeed in life,
make perseverance
your bosom friend,
experience your wise counselor,
caution your elder brother,
and hope your guardian genius.

Joseph Addison

The true measure of success is how many times you can bounce back from failure.

Stephen Richards

The way to get started is to quit talking and begin doing.

Walt Disney

Let no feeling of discouragement prey upon you, and in the end you are sure to succeed.

Abraham Lincoln

The greater danger for most of us
lies not in setting our aim
too high and falling short;
but in setting our aim too low,
and achieving our mark.

Michelangelo

The harder you fall,
the heavier your heart;
the heavier your heart,
the stronger you climb;
the stronger you climb,
the higher your pedestal.

Criss Jami

If you want to achieve excellence, you can get there today. As of this second, quit doing less-than-excellent work.

Thomas J Watson

Success is most often achieved by those who don't know that failure is inevitable.

Coco Chanel

Don't worry when you are not recognized, but strive to be worthy of recognition.

Abraham Lincoln

Success seems to be connected with action. Successful people keep moving. They make mistakes, but they don't quit.

Conrad Hilton

If you want to succeed you should
strike out on new paths,
rather than travel the worn paths
of accepted success.

John D. Rockefeller

A person has to remember that the road to success is always under construction. You have to get that through your head. That it is not easy becoming successful.

Steve Harvey

When you take risks you learn
that there will be times
when you succeed
and there will be times
when you fail,
and both are equally important.

Ellen DeGeneres

Stop chasing the money
and start chasing the passion.

Tony Hsieh

If you are willing to do more than you are paid to do, eventually you will be paid to do more than you do.

Anonymous

The ladder of success is best
climbed by stepping on
the rungs of opportunity.

Ayn Rand

Most people who succeed in the face of seemingly impossible conditions are people who simply don't know how to quit.

Robert H. Schuller

To succeed in life,
you need two things:
ignorance and confidence.

Mark Twain

I walk slowly,
but I never walk backward.

Abraham Lincoln

The great accomplishments
of man have resulted
from the transmission of ideas
and enthusiasm.

Thomas J. Watson

Genius is seldom recognized
for what it is:
a great capacity for hard work.

Henry Ford

All our dreams can come true,
if we have the courage
to pursue them.

Walt Disney

No man ever achieved worth-while success who did not, at one time or other, find himself with at least one foot hanging well over the brink of failure.

Napoleon Hill

I honestly think it is better to be a failure at something you love than to be a success at something you hate.

George Burns

If you set your goals ridiculously high and it's a failure, you will fail above everyone else's success.

James Cameron

The best thing about the future is that it comes one day at a time.

Abraham Lincoln

Though no one can go back and
make a brand new start,
anyone can start from now
and make a brand new ending.

Carl Bard

To see the list of other Your Daily Pill books on different topics, visit **www.yourdailypill.com**

www.ingramcontent.com/pod-product-compliance
Lightning Source LLC
Chambersburg PA
CBHW031404290426
44110CB00011B/257